The Scent of Flowers

A Journey Through Grief Healing and Love

by
Gloria Jean Roy

Published by Gloria Jean Roy
Woonsocket, Rhode Island

ISBN 1-57502-065-3

Printed in the USA by

MORRIS
PUBLISHING

3212 E. Hwy 30
Kearney, NE 68847
800-650-7888

Introduction

Although my sister, Gloria Jean Roy, has been writing poetry and short stories since she was very young, this book is her first publication.

The death of her beloved husband in 1993 generated these poems that came to her on a steady basis for several consistent months. This personal and heart-rending journey has enabled her to begin the process of healing and to once again find joy in living.

By generously sharing the private intimate details of her own desperate struggle through these inspirational poems, she hopes, when others are faced with similar difficult circumstances, they might at least find some comfort and solace in them.

Her steadfast courage, her indomitable strength and her constant perseverance is more than evident in these poems, and this book will undoubtedly become a formidable aid for those in bereavement who are fortunate to acquire it.

Patricia Roy Ladeira

*Dedicated
to the memory
of
my beloved husband*

~Gerald A. Roy~

With Sincere Thanks

To Doctor Thomas Steffens and Doctor Jon Dubois;

To Father Marcel Pincince who gave generously of his prayers and words of comfort;

To my parents, Leonard and Winifred Roy, for their support and my sister, Dianne Smith, for her many phone calls;

To Noel Pincince who stepped forward, gave me inspiration and love, and who always had faith in me;

To the St. Louis Choral for their beautiful music and songs never to be forgotten;

To WNRI with special thanks to Roger Bouchard, Donna Gallant and Romeo Berthiaume;

To Robert Picard, Tom Bouchard and The Hospice Care Program;

To my Granddaughter, Jennifer Roy, who told me every day that she loved me and that it was alright to cry;

To my friends, Muriel and Armand Dubois, Susan Moran Lague, Pete Picard, Eileen Faford, Germaine Fernandes, Marian Brodt;

To my Prince Charming, a special thank you for your caring, understanding and words of love;

And to all other family and friends, who in any way helped.

Special Recognition and Appreciation

To my sister, Patricia Roy Ladeira, for giving me the strength, courage and her devotion of always being there.

Preface

In May of 1986, I began a journey with my husband, Gerry, which lasted seven years. We had a wonderful love and were the best of friends, but our lives were suddenly shattered when my husband became seriously ill. He had developed a rare cancer, called Mesothelioma, which was fatal and was the direct result of asbestos exposure.

With tears in my eyes and a feeling of desperation, I went to my parish priest. He allowed me time alone in the church and I prayed harder than I had ever prayed before. I asked the Blessed Mother to give me one year with Gerry feeling well, so we could enjoy some quality time together, then I promised I would let him go. I felt consoled by loving feelings and overshadowed by a great power that I cannot explain. It was like a light around me - a touch of overwhelming inspiration - and it is difficult to express in words. I left the church with an odd feeling of happiness because I knew my prayers would be answered.

The next day Gerry was admitted to the New England Medical Center in Boston and had to undergo major surgery to remove the tumors in his abdomen area. This was a very slight chance of lengthening his life expectancy, but it was his only chance. Through the grace of God, Gerry made it through the surgery and became well again. He gradually began to gain weight and at his monthly check-ups the doctors in Boston were astonished at his remarkable recovery. They could not understand nor explain why he was improving so rapidly, but they knew that this was a very special case.

Every night my husband would say the rosary and a special prayer to St. Peregrine, the patron saint of cancer, and he continued to do well. His blood count was excellent, his vital signs were great, the cat scans came out negative, and they found no more cancer in his body. When he reached his first year after the surgery, I became nervous because of my deep promise to the Blessed Mother, but his good health remained for another five years. Although we tried to lived from day to day, we lived with the fear that the cancer would return. Each day that we awakened was a gift we truly treasured. Yet always there was this feeling of time, like a clock, quickly ticking away. Gerry and I would often talk about the cancer and what we would do if it returned. We both had great spiritual strength and believed that our situation was in God's hands. We were even surprised at how well he looked and how much energy he had. It was like nothing had ever happened. Could this be a miracle?

It was like a reprieve - a chance to live again. I thought then and believe now that it had to be the power of prayer. Our faith became stronger and we were thankful for our blessings every single day. To us, it was a miracle.

Then, in March of 1992, Gerry began to feel fatigued. He was admitted to the hospital and a biopsy was done on tissue from his chest cavity. A massive tumor was found between his heart and lungs. However, this time they would not perform surgery. Gerry and I agreed that he would try a low toxic chemotherapy, with the hope of slowing the tumor growth, and yet still giving him some quality time in his life. The chemotherapy treatments were extremely frightening. Our lives were up and down constantly, and from day to day Gerry would continue his struggle, while we kept our faith. Finally, in May of 1993, he faced his ultimate worse. He was admitted to the hospital again, this time to remove fluid from around his heart and lungs. He returned home and no longer could work. We both knew then that he was dying.

On June 3, 1993, Gerry became a patient of the Hospice Care Program, and his health began to steadily fail. He was confined to a wheelchair, a hospital bed and oxygen. We shared some very private times together. He was very emotional, telling me it was his time to go to God but that I had to stay. I wept and asked him if he would promise to wait for me at the "gate". He said he would wait with open arms, provided I stayed behind. I promised him in return that I would.

On the morning of June 29, 1993, due to the long night by Gerry's bedside, I decided to take a shower to refresh myself. My sister, Patricia, and my sister-in-law, Janet, stayed with Gerry. After my shower, I was dressing and suddenly felt a need to rush downstairs to be with my husband. When I walked into the room, it was completely joyous. Gerry's eyes were sparkling and opened wide and his face appeared youthful - I felt wonderful. I went to his bedside smiling and said, "Hi Gerry!" At that moment, he closed his eyes, touched me, and died. I was overwhelmed with grief as I put my arms around him and held him close to me. Then my sister and sister-in-law left the room, and I abruptly stopped crying. There was no pain from grief and I knew Gerry was at peace. I experienced an aroma of flowers from his body which gave me great comfort and joy. As I continued to smell his body for this aroma, I felt like I was completely in another world and not alone. The Scent of Flowers penetrated the room and lasted until I was interrupted by the nurse a short time later. This experience gave me the strength I needed to face my sons, enlightenment to go on, and gratitude to God for granting us the gift of life to share with one another a little longer. I believe in God and His gifts and I will never forget the Scent of Flowers.

Through inspiration, I started to write these poems to help relieve some of the pain of grieving. The poems I have written allowed me to heal and to express my silenced feelings of love. This was a journey I had to complete, so I could begin to live once again.

The Scent of Flowers

Sweet The Day

A bridal wreath of roses
The vows we speak - our words of love
A snow white gown of grace
Angels flying high above
Sweet the day!
The crimson color of your lips
To kiss the one I love
The sparkling ring placed on my finger
To bond to life forever
Sweet the day!
Candles glow and anxiously we wait
To say the words I do
This unforgotten moment at the altar
Shall be a vision - I will cherish of you
Sweet the day!
Till death do we part
It is only a start
To grow our love
Into the gate - you will wait
Sweet the day!

Honeymoon

How would you talk
About a honeymoon?
A paradise of love!
A secret hide-a-way!
A cold crisp evening.
Dinner for two.
We toast champagne
With a kiss or two.
An evening of satin and lace
In a world of our own
A reward for our love.
I feel like a young child
With a shyness blush.
A maiden of innocence
With a feeling of trust.
The unity of the two of us.

Sons

So long I wait
For the birth of our first child
Finally I hear the cry.
How proud we are
Born to us a beautiful son!
Two years later - once again
Our second son is born.
A blessing from above!
Four years past now
Surprise! Our third son is born.
You stood so tall for our sons
Proudness you showed
For your name to carry on.
Our little boys of fun and joy
How fast they grew.
Down the road - two more sons
Adopted from our love so strong.
Our sons - no longer boys
So bold! So brave!
I see your smile
In all of them.

Silver Year

A celebration of sterling satin
Shimmering like a silvery moon
Across the vast ocean.
The playful waves bounce
With glorious perfection
Wandering from the sunset
To the sandy shore.
Toast the wine
To a silver year of time.
Enchantment is our love
Never forgotten.
Our trust in faith
Our dreams of love
Have softened our years to blossom
Into this silver celebration
To remember with love forever.

A Little Miracle

What do you mean that I am going to die?
Have you no pity for me?
I can hear all that you are saying.
I cannot believe it is happening to me!
I give myself to God
To find a way for me to stay
Just a little longer -
To love my darling wife
And to share with my sons
A little more of my life.
Just a little miracle -
A blessing from Thee -
To have, to hold,
To give of myself endlessly.
Thank you, for thinking twice,
And giving me additional time
For those I adore in my life.
The chain of prayers is working for me.
I can feel your strong affection -
A thankful gift that I received
From the God I love.

The Rosary

Every night I watch you pace
From room to room to say your rosary.
For seven years, I wait for you
To finish your prayers
With deep relief.
Is this why you survived?
What promise did you make?
Was it thanks
That made you live so long?
Is it a hidden secret?
Or did you dwell in a dream?
Did you see her?
Your prayers were so abundant
They awakened you to search for hope.
Each bead of prayer
You spoke in French
And your eyes were unopened.
Light shines from your rosary.
And your prayers were answered.
Your faith - is why you lived!

The Meeting

Here we are - our final meeting
Family gathered around!
Listen to the words
That they are speaking.
There are no strangers seeking.
Feel the love and the wisdom
Understand! For I am leaving!
No goodbyes - No teary eyes
Are there any questions?

This Man - A King

This man - is he a King?
He looks so weary and so thin.
Thru somber days of painful sin
He breathes so shallow and limp.
Yet he stands with pride
And always gives a smile.
He lives in his home.
He clings.
Feel the earth move
Feel the rainbow of colors surround you.
My King! My King!
Your crown goes forth.
Your triumph will soon end
And forever, your reign will begin.

Watch And Wait

Each day I watch you grow so helpless.
By your bedside, I pray.
With promises of life above
I do not know what to say
But can only express my love.
Can I live and bear my sorrow?
I watch and I wait in vain.
The hour of the moment will pass
Like a night wind
Of a storm that came to an end.
I pace, I cry, I linger
For one moment more.
I sit and hold your hand.
I kiss your lips with calmness.
I know I will miss you
But I must let you go
Into another life of eternal rest.

The Last Days

In your lasting days
You spoke words of your death.
You told me that Jesus
Was deeply within you.
You said it was your turn to go and
I must stay - you made me promise.
I asked, "Will you meet me at the gate?"
You smiled and said, "With open arms!"
The love of your feelings
You gave to all of us.
You touched every part of me
Because you cared.
We never said goodbye - no need.
You are just behind another door.
A door that will open
When I get there.

The Gift

Enter the room for joy
Feel the silent peace.
I held you in my arms
To cry many tears
I had to release.
My body had no pain.
I felt a golden light
A light that shone upon us
Into the daylight.
The comfort we shared.
The flowers in a field
The freshest scent taken
Into my heart with no more tears.
Oh! How I believe the gift you sent to me
Of lasting love
To grow into a new world
Of solemn peace.

Lady Of Wonder

From heaven with a holy flame
A mother descends - her freedom extends.
A beauty of mystical power
She walked into your life
Like a blue shining knight.
A halo adorns her head.
With music from harps
Silent thunder in a twilight fire
She cast her power with desire.
A maiden's heart to feel love
Upon her white throne
Embraced by glory.
A path of stairs to a lighted tower
You join forever to a lady of wonder.
Set forth - shout a new joy
Into a beauty of new birth to endure.

The Faded Rose

The first rose of summer
Alone to bloom
Shall soon be faded and gone.
The petals fall on the ground
Leaving the stem to scatter.
The gem of the rose smells so sweet
Like friends who gather to weep
Lonely with disbelief.
The widow cries out with grief
But the spirit of the rose shall mourn
With the rhythm of a song so true and tender
To the beat of her heart.
It is splendor!

Memories And Love Never Die

A man of sunshine to bring a smile
A man of words for laughter of tears
A caring man - a family man
A man of courageous spirit and faith.
He believed in miracles and he succeeded.
He beat the odds with good will and God.
He was a character with surprise remarks.
He touched so many lives.
He was my best friend.
He loved me deeply.
Lucky me! I got to marry him!

Laid To Rest

On a satin pillow
You rest your head.
You sleep so deep in peace.
Your body so cold
As I kiss your lips
And say I love you
Oh! How I wish you could speak.
You lay in a shadow box of solid oak
With Jesus on your side.
A heart of flowers I give to you
With an American flag not far away.
A veteran you are.
You will be laid to rest
Under golden gravel.
Your body - a shell
For you have gone on
With power and dignity
To live forever.

Let It Be

In God's house, I feel so loved.
Friends from many paths of life
To give, to share
An expression of deep sympathy.
Voices praise His holy name!
The spirit of His being is by my side.
His presence is here - I see a light so bright.
Tears of sorrow yet the glory is all around.
Let it be.
The steps we take - are a very short journey.
You were there, with a joyous smile.
You march triumphantly.

All That I Could

Why are you here?
Your name pressed on a stone
A grave of sadness.
Do you feel alone?
The flowers lay on the grass
While ribbons of satin
Move with the wind.
You were so young!
I feel my world closing in.
Why was it taken from thee?
Will I ever be the same?
Will I ever live without pain?
My Darling! I did all that I could.

The Warrior

The thunder of the drums
A battle you won
How brave the warrior you are!
You heard the bugles.
Hark! To the mighty sound.
Go forth! New joy awaits you.
A hero of faith, victory at last
March on with your sword.
Rejoice! Wave the flag.
The truth of a soldier
Now enters the heavens above.

Hallow Night

My bed has grown
So large and empty
No warmth by my side.
I sleep into a hallow night.
I dream light, my eyes filled with tears.
Sighing and wishing
Praying and sobbing
Until I feel no fear.
Then in the dim gray light of morn
I arise from the glare
Of the brilliant sun.
Gone are the moments that we planned.
Those sweet days.
The turn of the seasons
Now have deeper reasons.

The Robe

These tangible things you left behind
The robe you wore so tattered with time.
The diamond, the gold
That real bright tie!
Perfume, lotion, that crazy little something!
The pictures of the times we shared are fading.
Where do they go? What do I do?
All these treasures
Do I destroy?
Childhood toys, teen idols
That ugly sweater that drove me wild?
Pack them - give them to the poor.
They are gone forever.
Your robe not never!

What Happened

What happened to me?
I have so much pain.
It is like a snake devouring me.
I cannot breathe - I cannot sleep.
So confused! Which way to go?
Some days, the sun shines.
Rainy days, bring me tears.
How can this be?
How could you die without me?
I never really thought it would end.
Not now - too young to go.
Living forever is not a promise.
I know my pain will leave.
I grieve, I scream, I cry
But our love will never die.

I'm Home

Honey! I'm home!
Are you hiding on me?
What room are you in?
What do you mean you are not here?
Okay! I will close my eyes
Just for a minute
Then I know you will be here.
You mean you died?
But why? It cannot be.
I thought you loved me.
What did I hear? I am alone
To grow old
But when will that be?

The Red White And Blue

My first holiday without you
It is a celebration
Of the red, white and blue.
My flag is at half-staff
No wind to make it wave.
There is no sound of fireworks
A silence remains.
It is so solemn, this fourth of July
The children are here, but from them I am apart.
No soldiers to march on my parade
It stopped - the weapons have dropped.
A mist of blue - no song or tune
The day is hot but only cold I feel.
A grave illumination
Of the red, white and blue.

The Cross I Bear

A heavy heart has no sun
Repose in vain is my pain.
I lay alone with deep regret
And feel remorse I will never forget -
Bringing silent memories of the past
To reach and search with a pleasant glow.
Oh! Solemn the day I stored away
Everlasting love we enjoyed.
Courage still - alone will I dream
To fantasize the blossoms of Spring.
The cross I bear with love and fear
And with wondrous strength
I will treasure through many years.

Sleep

Sleep, my Love, Sleep.
The flowers have died
The trees are bare
Summer nights have disappeared.
The day grows weary into a slumber night
So calm - so deep
A lonesome midnight at a peek.
Heavenly signs slip through my mind
As deep into rest
Hopes and fears diminish.
Silent the day and parting pain
Love only surrounds you.
Sleep, my Love, Sleep.
You are now at peace.

No Reflection

Under the evening sky
The glorious roses have died.
My features not the same
But like dead leaves
That have drifted away.
No blushing color, no pigment in my lips,
No reflection in the mirror -
I stare but no one is there.
No sound of music, no voices singing
Deep silence is ringing from my mind -
Crushing of stones on my bosom
I wonder why I am still living.
Only death warms me now
Because I know, I could be with you.
How dark is this hour that will pass
To guide me into a new lighted path.

Fear

Yes, my Dear, I am here.
Still searching
Since you disappeared.
I reach for hope.
I dig and seek.
Still wondering why
This happened to me.
My brain is weak
And my heart trembles.
I have no cares - I weep.
I am defeated
And feel so incomplete.
I do not think I want to live.
I declare - I have much fear.
Time to say a prayer.

No Answers

I cannot ever wonder why
There are no answers - no replies.
I cannot question why you died
But still I send you my love.
In the sunlight of the day
I dream of holding you tight.
I will never say goodbye
Just be there to greet me when I die.
You will always be my true love
And deep inside of me our memories I will hold.
I suppose I have to learn to live without you.
But I will love you forever
And I know that I will see you again.

Never Give Up

With courage you lived well -
Your laughter and love filled our lives.
Our children learned the power of strength -
Respect - with honor on a pedestal.
You gave your best with inspiration -
Long into my mind - the memories.
Your death pierced my heart -
So pitiful with sad thoughts.
You taught me never to give up -
To search for hope - to find peace
And to carry on with faith.

Only You

I see you in a vision.
You follow me each day.
You touch me and I am deeply moved.
Your tenderness remains.
A love beyond - but it is gone.
Our love was a love
You do not find every day.
You cast a shadow
Like the glow from a candle -
With this I will get by.
For only you gave me
A reason for living, giving
And, yes, a way of dying.

Last Dance

A short time has passed away
Yet in my mind you stay.
Are you really there? The music plays.
You seem to be with me today.
I feel you around me.
Do not go!
Please let me know -
Show me that you are here.
Am I playing a game?
My heart tells me you are here.
You made me smile - whispered my name.
Hear our song -
Dance this last dance with me.
Do not leave - stay -
Dance before you stray.

A Messenger

What are you doing here?
This cannot be.
What did you say?
You had to see me because you missed me?
It is great to see you!
Oh my! You are a ghost.
I must be dreaming or is this a hoax?
My son, did you see him?
Did you hear him speak?
Look! He is here.
Can you not see?
He is smiling at me.
Look again! He is gone.
Please do not leave.
Oh! I see! It is a messenger - I believe.

You And Me

Between you and me
There is just a white light-
A line for me to cross.
A measure of time -
Smoky blue clouds -
A pillar of pearls -
Unknown to the world -
Tremendous sorrow, we must part.
Embraced by a love we had -
Can life still be the best?
Why do you rest?
The space between you and me
Is larger than I could ever believe.
The gate is so heavy
Is it made of gold?
Slowly I die in a darkened sky
To be an angel for thee.

Fatherhood

You taught a lesson in fatherhood
Respect from your sons you abundantly received.
Those strange ways of discipline -
Frenzied and wild -
Are now remembered with ease.
Frightened they may have been
But honor was their dignity.
Knowing right from wrong
They believed you were strong.
Never disappointed -
They cherished your name.
A man of his word, who never complained
A devoted father, a best friend.

A Star So Bright

Dream on and look around
Do you see?
Lights that twinkle - stars shining bright
Listen to the song of a winter night.
The birth of a Savior -
Happy faces in a crowd -
Hear the tinkling of the bells ringing
The reverence in the choir's singing.
Perhaps you are a shepherd with a staff
Following a radiant star.
Gifts surround the tree
But your name is missing.
A first Christmas without you - so empty.
Yet it is your first Christmas
In a world of beauty -
A heaven of many family and friends.
Please sprinkle a little dust from above.
Merry Christmas - My Love!

The Worse

This is the worse - it is agony.
I am a turtle in a shell -
A trapped animal in a cage -
I am frantic every day.
Will anyone understand me?
I do not feel fulfilled.
It is strange - sometimes I panic.
How can someone with love be destroyed?
I have gone from a princess in a castle
To a shadow of misery -
From fertile seed to barren ashes.
Will my life ever be bountiful again?
Will I ever find serenity?
Can I ever be consoled?

Family Life

Family life is not the same
Since you passed away.
The image of you is now a black scar
Pressed into my heart.
The wholeness - the goodness -
The solid frame is gone.
How do I begin to build a new home
That can be bright and fun?
Do I start from the foundation?
Work my way up - is this the form?
Or do I die and leave behind
The tears and sorrow
For others to carry on?

Home So Sweet

Warm little home -
Touch of elegance -
Colors of pastel so pure -
A welcome mat at the door -
Pot of tea for you and me -
Flowers and potpourri!
Love is all around
Yet I am totally alone.
This home so sweet
Adorned with pictures so elite.
Pillows accent the decor -
Full of cheer!
I wish you were here.
This charming home
Would be happy for two
But alas this home will be
Forever - just for me.

A New Year

May old acquaintances be forgot.
How can that be?
I cannot forget - but I do forgive thee.
You pardoned yourself with grace.
A New Year - new beginnings -
Will I have a new life?
The ball drops - it is midnight.
No lips to kiss - no toast to wish -
No balloons - party horns - smiling faces -
The glitter and sparkle is all gone.
I enter the New Year alone.
Will my pain ever disappear?

Burning Love

Often when I am feeling low
I speak the words I love to hear
Like "Your the best!"
"You look so wonderful!"
"God is with you, my dear."
I visualize your smile.
I even see you walk in from your daily work.
I have searched for help
And read the book of Wisdom.
I felt the touch.
I will never forget the love
By the light you left.
The gentle glow is sweeter
Than the wine we shared.
Forever instilled in my heart -
A burning love for an eternal fire of desire.

Time Will Pass

No matter what I do
No matter what I say
I feel your heart beating
Inside me every day -
But only for one moment
Could you kiss my pain away.
I shall not show any weakness
But will build on your strength and pray
For power to continue
Every single day.
I will win a victory and I will do
What must be done each day.
Though I am shattered now
Like a broken piece of glass
This time will pass
And the shadow of my doubts will go away.
Then I will know that you will not return
But deep down within my heart you will stay.

Love Bird

Guess what my Love?
I have company.
A little lovebird
That chirps in my ear.
He thinks I am his mother
And he surely loves me dear.
A pleasant guest who never rests
And green with a peach face.
He can be silly and sometimes mean.
I spoil him - I give him treats -
This crazy lovebird cannot speak.
Still alone - but he helps.
Someone to say hello to
When I come home.

Do You Know

Do you ever wonder why you died?
Do you know that you left without me?
Do you know that I have pain? It hurts all the time.
Do you know that I am lost? Where do I go?
Do you know that I am sad? My smile no longer there.
Do you know that I cry each and every day?
Do you know that I miss you? Emptiness fills my heart.
Do you know that I am lonely? You are not here to love.
Do you know that I am cold? No more warmth inside.
Do you ever wonder what happened to me?
I am still here struggling to get by.

The Wedding Ring

No wedding ring on my finger!
No longer marriage to you -
An empty ring finger.
Just pearls I wear
As tears of pain for you.
The impression of my wedding ring
Still around my finger
Looks strange.
I remember the day you placed it there -
Your eyes were filled with tears
From the powerful love you had for me.
The gold ring came with vows to never let go.
The wedding ring - a symbol of love!
The emblem of your love
Will always remain
Imprinted upon my soul.

Godly Incident

Were you there?
It did not look like you.
Much of him was similar -
His smile - his wit -
His manner was it.
I suppose for a moment
I wished it was you.
You leave slight traces -
A salt shaker - a drink -
The number game you played!
A person in a crowd
Resembled you.
I heard your voice - I swear!
My mind must have played a trick -
My imagination of a situation.
Was it just a memory?
Was it a coincidence?
Or was it a Godly incident?

Missing You

In the wee hours of the morning
I miss you most of all -
My world is so restless without you.
Our love of so long ago -
To me - within my heart - seems to have just begun.
I see you in my dreams
And I feel you in my arms.
Falling in love was to be forever!
Can I really give my heart to anyone else?
Perhaps! Only time can do the telling.

Passion Of Love

Cold was the moment
You were taken away from my arms
To love beyond.
A defeat that ends
With desolate ways of self
Crushed into a burning fire of desire.
One more touch to feel the warmth
Of your passionate love.
To be with you as one
Intimate and close -
As a rose clings to a vine
Together forever.
But you had to part
Leaving me like a dying blaze
Drifting smoke into clouds above.
What do I do?
Where do I go?
And most of all
Will I ever love again?

Heartache

I cannot get over the loss of you.
The pain is too great.
It is unbelievable heartache!
I cannot pretend I am doing well -
It is really a game that I play.
I want to hold you
Just once more.
My lips whisper - "I love you so!"
But you are not here -
I am so alone.
It was a light
That took you away.
I say to myself -
What more can I do?
All I know is I want you.

Endless Time

I see the day through a haze.
I am a martyr of a persecution
I cannot explain.
An arrow with a point so sharp
It penetrated my heart.
My inner feelings are of death
Since you left.
I shake my head with disbelief and astonishment.
Can this truly be?
A chance to take -
With love to give - just has to be.
One of us had to go first -
One of us had to remain behind.
I do believe I will receive.
Our love will be with endless time -
No pain - only heaven to gain.

Wander To A Path

Look at me! How sad can I be?
A wandering person lost at sea.
A weeping willow - white as a dove
Bound to let pale wings fly
Beyond a perishing breeze.
Sweet hopes - bitter pain -
Indefinite hours that last yet pass.
Until I see you again
My soul will whisper
Of all its dreams in splendor.
The cherished hour of joyous life
That brought only a darkness bright.
Step by step
I will wander to a path
That will set me free.

One Of A Kind

You were original -
One of a kind!
No model from where you came.
You were here
For merely a short time
But you achieved
A great reality.
You tickled everyone's fancy
And no animosity could be found.
You impressed with your kindness -
Soft - gentle to the touch -
Never a streak of malice.
You did it the genteel way
With faith, love and trust -
Willing to share with all of us.

I Miss Me

I laughed today. Should I feel guilty?
How can I be happy? After all, you are dead.
When I see two people in love
Holding hands and kissing
I am disturbed with extreme jealousy.
I find no comfort around lovers.
Why are they together?
It should be us instead.
My feelings of passion - obsessed with anger
Like a baby bird without his mother.
This inner side that tears at me
Is only a temporary unkind thought.
I sometimes have two personalities.
I am living in a misty fog.
I miss me - the way I use to be.
But some day - somewhere -
I will awaken at a doorstep
To find myself home - with love at last.

My Poem To You

I am writing this little poem
So you will know
I think of you each day.
Oh! Angel! My sweet Angel!
Although thee I cannot see,
I sense the comfort of your spirit
Ever near to me.
No power beyond a stormy sea
Can take away what will always be.

Love Letters

I took a peek at love letters
Of so many years ago.
The words that were written then -
Of our young love - did show.
The kind words of value and trust
So precious to me, my Love.
I paused for a moment
To reread your expressions of love-
To bring back the memories
That lovers always quote.
Oh! How I remember so well
The passing of our secret codes.
We had so many.
Where did those years go?
Those wonderful love letters
I will forever hold dear.
Pretty notes and special memories
To carry always and to never let go.

Beautiful Stallion

I sat upon a painted horse
And rode into a bright sunlight.
The colors were vivid
As they glowed and glittered.
The painted horse became so old
That all the colors turned to gold.
A prince appeared on a beautiful stallion
And he was not old, alone or tired.
He lifted me like a feather in the breeze
And we rode into a misty blue night.
My prince held me close and swept me away -
It was a lovely heavenly sight.

Soul Mates

A hush of words and wings that flutter
Halo beams into the night -
And I hear your voice with loving delight.
The garden full of daffodils!
The gate with your illuminated face!
I know you will be there
With laughter so bold
At the road that will lead me
To the gate that unfolds.
A spirit gleaming - sad memories will end.
Beauty and joy will open the door
And together again our souls will mate.

My Angel

There is an angel near
For I feel the wings beneath me.
The vision I see
Has love unconditionally.
I feel my angel holding me -
A beautiful angel -
Who hugs and kisses my tears away.
My angel weeps
When I have sad days -
But embraces me and carries me
When I am in pain.
A spirit not seen
Who protects and guides me -
Sent from heaven above
From the God I love.
Never a day will my angel not pray -
The angel I love
Is with me in every way.

Will It Ever Be

Will I ever win? Can it ever be?
Just a sign I ask to help me.
It is gone forever. How do I fight?
Is it possible? Am I becoming weak?
Into the hands of the enemy
With no team to meet -
A lost soul in a battle
With no glory to be.
No salvation - no strike against force
A storm with no protection from the high seas.
Will it ever be? Will it ever end?
Will I at last win this victory?

It Won

Beautiful morn
Sun so strong
Yet black clouds all around -
Once again, it won!
A time of grief
Smiles turned into tears -
You weep and fall into a tunnel
That spins and twirls.
It is black magic - evil with spite
It is not alright.
Only memories can dig so deep
Into a pit so steep.
Push the tarrying pain away
Fluff the tearful pillow of white -
Cry out and be bold.
It has been told.

A Prayer

I said a prayer for you today
To ask the Lord to guide you in every way
To grant you peace and love within
To keep you happy in his glorious kingdom.
The light that sparks
In the heavenly skies
Shines upon your soul.
And so I asked -
With his power so great
Our Father from above -
Keep a special place in heaven
For the man I love.
Please answer my pray -
My Lord! My God! -
And send me your wonderful love of hope.

With No Trace

Alone I walked along the sea shore.
I held a pearly shell in my hand
And wrote your name in the sand.
A wave rolled in and washed your name away.
Like the tide comes in and out -
So our lives begin and end -
With no trace of ourselves
A moment in time to erase.
So strong the waves
So weak we stand
From sea to shore
A mortal part of the glory we adore.

Old Clock

The clock is still ticking in my room
A reminder of time and days of doom.
This old clock with its old springs
I wind at the close of each day.
It was your treasure and pride
And it never will die.
Ninety years old - it will still tick away
Chiming on the hour.
It will never stop, muffle or sway.
Such a joy that old clock -
Its beauty like a ring of gold.
The pendulum swings to and fro -
Never a second to be old -
Tick - tick - tick - it never will go!

The Insane Widow

Do you know that widows are insane?
They can be happy and sad all in one day.
They can look strong but really are weak -
You would not know - the widow hides it so deep.
They can even comfort you and make you glad.
Widows do silly things and say crazy words
That will drive you mad.
Up one day - down another!
The widow will make you cry
But her tears will never shed.
She makes you worried and confused.
You will find her poor
But then observe her on a shopping spree.
She travels across the seas.
She buys herself gifts of gold and diamonds.
The widow will shrug it off.
When she acts strangely, you will wonder to yourself
There she goes - shopping again!
What do you think?
Has the widow given you a bite
Or are you going to pass it out of sight?
Poor little widow does not care
Lost in a stew - life has no fear.
Do you believe the widow is really insane?
Think again - she has terrible pain.

Beautiful Joy

The terrible dark will go away
The day I die for you.
My soul will touch the sun for its gentle warmth
And my dreams will begin to sing
With raging fire in my heart - as I grow old.
Oh! How I yearn to be with thee!
The laughter of the years
Will start to ring.
Tender words we will speak
As we stroll to Paradise.
Beautiful joy will open the door
And our life as one will begin.

Like Death

I have grieved in every season -
In hot summer winds
Under a colorful autumn sun
Through a winter of snow
And the spring of a blushing rose.
The year has past
And the pity I experienced
Was worse than a terrifying storm.
The affliction of pain
Was excruciating to the touch.
The frosty chill of my feelings
Was like death -
Characteristic of a grave
Every step of the way.
The first year of agony has left.

Friendship

A few words can fade away
But a smile - a tear - a thank you
Will last for much more than a year -
So I grin and give you all my cheers.
Teardrops I have but in my heart
I know all of you genuinely care.
I say thank you for the heavenly sounds
Thank you for the friendship we share
And - most of all -
I say thank you for being there
During my most painful year.

Can You Feel

You are dead, my Dear.
Do I sing a sad song?
Do I praise or weep at your grave?
Have you forgotten me?
Do I wilt like an old rose?
Did my heart go with you?
Will you rise to see me once again?
If I speak, do you hear?
Can you feel the grass above?
Can you feel the rain or dewdrops?
Should I plant flowers around your stone?
I know you are not here but in heaven above.
You did not forget.
No regrets!
I will see you again one day.

Close To Letting Go

Where do I begin? I cannot say goodbye
But I will say, "See you later."
I am close to letting you go - it is time.
I will miss you -
And I already sense that you are not around.
How long will I live? Will I grow old?
Will I meet someone - who is not you -
And will I love again?
It hurts! I did not want this.
It is ended. Nothing I can do.
I will see you again in another time.
You will be there. It is faith I know.
I am sorry I cannot be with you any more.
Since I am here, I have to be happy - that is me.
You remember? I always laughed and smiled -
Just like you.
I hate this - I never will say goodbye.
You will always be in my heart and soul.
Do you know I cannot stop crying?
I will try to do my best.
Just remember -
I will love you forever.

Tomorrow

Today I feel I can endure
As the earth seems
Like a better place.
I smiled and felt the sun
Light up my face
And I spoke of you
With words of grace.
My home of roses has bloomed
Into a happy dwelling of my own.
I imagine you by my side
Letting me be free to wander
And to find some joy for me -
But my world is not always bright.
Have that firelight waiting
To show me the way to go -
I have tomorrow you know.

Freedom

Do not bother me for I live alone -
I am independent you know.
My freedom I have so do not interrupt.
Did you not hear? I am liberated at last.
I still have pain with no gain
But wisdom and caring I also have.
No mistakes shall I make.
I will take care of myself
And you will have to wait.
I do not cook and I sleep late.
I do what I want - come home when I please -
And never think twice when I purchase some things.
I have supper alone - bologna or cheese.
Yet I still have love to give away.
Maybe some day a man will enter my life.
I will let him charm and dine me.
No strings attached!
It is alright. Do not worry.
I am getting there.
Have you not heard?

A Kite

I make believe that you are a kite
And I am holding the string
As you fly high in the sky.
Do you not see?
You are still attached to me.
My fingers are paralyzed.
I must pull the string
And let you go. When I decide!
Though I must admit -
I have released a little bit.
Some day I will let you fly away.
I just do not know
When that day will be.

Courage

I pulled myself together
For a day with no tears.
This bright mood
Of thinking of you
Escapes my widowhood.
I am courageous!
My heart beats like a lion
Yet I am still fragile
Like a china doll.
My world opened today
And I saw a lovely linen sky -
The image of you
Always by my side.

Inspiration

An inspiration was given to me
And it was a considerable gift -
A cloud over me
That burst into tears and mist.
It came from power beyond
From a beautiful lady of blue
And it gives me grand pleasure
To share this exceptional view.
From scarlet red to dusty pink
The colors of a rainbow -
Or a sunset of golden dew -
All colors giving love.
A nature of existing - a way of expressing.
Use the gifts that you receive
To share with others in unity.
Bless the power and be understood.
Thankful graces - a bounty to thee -
The gift you accept shall be counted.
Inspiration - a way of living your life
On a journey to paradise.

Time

A grieving pain overwhelms you -
It is so deep you cannot sleep.
Your body trembles
And your heart gets weak.
You often wonder if you will make it -
Fighting is the remedy.
Talking, sharing, never denying -
Even hopeful is kind and you must try.
This time you will find
Your most loyal friends.
One day at a time -
One minute - one moment to survive -
Tears, screams, pacing -
It is alright.
Overshadowed, confused and downhearted -
Keep faith in yourself
And take one step at a time!
Reach out for help
From those who show care.
Believe me -
You will make it - you will succeed -
Time is what you really need.

A Bad Scene

I cannot be by your side.
How do I forgive you?
How dare you leave me
To deal with everything alone?
No more love
To set our world on fire.
No more love
To willingly share with each other.
I am free.
I thought we would be forever
And would part this world together -
But it was your time - not mine - to go.
My time is still to be here - alone.

Wake Up

The songs are old
And twilight time has passed.
Only he - cheated my heart -
But I will not fall apart.
Do not deceive yourself
Time is not costly.
Live fully in this world
It is yours to keep.
Memories are now a fortune!
You have new places to go -
New people to meet -
And hardened hearts are for those so cold.
Click your heels and go.
Master your own mind
And set yourself free -
No longer live in agony.
Wake up! It is daylight -
Breathe - walk - do not run.
The day will vanish quickly
As you should know.

Adored

Oh! How we danced!
It is a new romance
And you held me close.
You spoke words
Sweetly tender and in tune.
I felt desirable
And beautiful again
Like a package with a bow.
How you adored me
From my finger tips to my toes.
Our love to dance -
So wonderful!

Quality Love

A possessing power
Of a water stream
Flows from my eyes -
Uncontrolled and hidden inside.
Will there ever be
An absolution of grace
To release my thoughts -
And to forget this tragic scene
Of emptiness and loneliness?
For now, I am a specialist
Of grief, sorrow, and heartfelt pain.
Yet - I must remember -
The quality of our love
Can never be erased.

A Branch Of A Tree

A piece of wood cast away
Once belonged to a foundation -
A beautiful tree of green -
A tree standing tall with dignity.
A tree has a personality
Like a person
Giving you shade for protection.
Climb the tree and look for a bird's nest -
This tree can be a home.
A tree branches out
And will lose a limb in the wind -
Taking some small branches with it -
As when we leave this life
Forsaking someone we love.
Yet the piece of wood still has its own beauty!
Like the tree, we branch away
Leaving behind our love, our memories, our tears
To grow into eternal happiness.
Go forth, give love, share - touch someone forever!
Have faith and always
Branch out for one another.

A Positive Mind

Alright! I will accept it.
Where do I go from here
To start my day with no tear?
No choices - no decisions-
Just a mission -
A positive mind -
To think only yes!
Am I captive or chained?
Do I set myself free?
Unburden this quest -
Do not hasten - do not quiver
Be swift and finish it.
Bad days will go away -
Bring me only a holiday.
Get on the starting line
And be ready -
You must make it to your goal.
Make it a "plus" day
A "pleasant" day
Or even just a "yes" day.

The Perfect Day

Shout a new joy!
Praise for victory!
Today is a day I have lived.
I saw the blue sky -
The sun shining high -
And I heard the birds sing.
The grass is greener than
My perfect daydream.
The air is so fragile -
The flowers smell sweet.
I have found myself!
I was concealed behind an ivy
Climbing and clinging
To a stone wall -
But I broke away
From it all.
I picked up my head
Stood on my own two feet -
And strutted along with a smile
As I marched down the street.

I Fly Unguarded

It is my life to live again.
All of its strength appeals to me.
Happy - I listen to praise -
But I do keep a secret
Wretched in my soul.
For me - it is never to be told.
I fly unguarded - a moment in time.
My ears can still hear
The many words you spoke.
Many are the friends who share
Laughter or a tear.
My time is precious.
I know what I read.
Fighting back - going ahead -
Time is now - life is here -
Traveling forward - indeed I will.
My trembling road is now still.

Who Can Help

In time of need -
In sorrow and grief -
Who can help or comfort me?
A sister - who listens intently.
A mother - who loves you unconditionally.
A friend - who stands by your side.
All sharing so I can get by.
How lucky can I be - to have all three!
I can cope - I can smile -
Because they care so much for me.

Back Home

I see your face everywhere -
By the mystic sea
In a fire by a hearthstone
Even in an opened flower.
From you - no escape for me.
It is like something holy
Pursuing me.
It seems real - not a fairytale -
Nor a dream I have in vain.
Even the songs of yesteryear
Do not part from me.
It is an overcast
That never leaves.
It strongly upsets me!
My constant wish is this -
That you were back home with me.

On My Own

My hands are folded against time and fate
Eager to know which way to go
To be free from my misery.
I struggle with the want of one more kiss.
I will do my best to make you proud of me.
As a rosebud slow to bloom, I shall be -
Or as an angel waiting to gain wings.
I will stand for truth above the earth
With a gaze of life to master -
A song in my heart, planted by a single note,
Always praying that I will make it on my own.

Lost

In my shoes
You would feel blue.
No place to run or hide
From the terrible pain inside.
Shakened - Lost - Tranquil Thoughts -
A complex matter
That cannot be forgot.
Will I ever be complete again?
To think again?
To be just me again?
Only time will bring to me
A feeling of reaching high
To show the greatest pride.

Midnight Dream

Sitting silent within my mind
I collect the thoughts
Of a midnight dream.
You never spoke a word -
Just waved from a boat
And smiled with lots of hope.
You jumped into
The clean crystal water
And swam the backstroke.
The graceful white boat floated away
And all you did was wave.
I cannot touch you or speak to you.
Does this dream mean
That you are far away?
Or did you just want to let me know
That you are really okay?

Forever Young

Petals of a flower
A scent of perfume
A potpourri of fuchsia color
From red coral to crimson heather.
Sage leaves, prickly thorns and seeds
Blowing into the wind
Bringing life back into me.
Beneath a shady tree
Or in a garden budding
There is tranquility.
The funny face of a pansy makes me smile -
Reminding me of a loved one long ago.
Green grass, ferns, and ivy
Wild country in an untamed meadow -
Forever young in heart
You will never part.
It is no secret -
Life is a love affair
If you are smart.

Your Wishes

My Angel! I have tried.
Do not be saddened -
Your sons miss you very much.
They cannot see ahead
To your happy dream -
A peaceful garden
In a valley called heaven.
The will you had to live so long -
Beyond the tide of destiny - ended.
You had to leave.
No choice! You had to perceive.
I promise to keep
The wishes you wanted
For me to continue to believe.

Unimaginable Flight

Time passes calmly
As I rock in an old oak chair
To an odyssey of an unimaginable flight.
I see you everywhere.
Soothing - relaxing
Ever present in my mind
I can smell the lotion that you wore.
Awkward silence - I do not hear.
I feel a blushing of heat within myself -
A blessing in despair.
Surprisingly pleasant here -
Like seeds planted to grow
Into a sunflower or a yellow rose -
A lovelight of a passage to home -
A visit in the call of the night.
It is wonderful to know
That I can feel you are near.

Good Times

Glory be forgot!
I shall not.
I remember.
The beauty that you gave
And the good times we rocked away.
We played - we loved -
We laughed to tears -
And even some secrets we shared.
Slaves to love but we did not care.
Never any fancy expressions
Only a slogan of frolic words.
You shone like a star
In yonder heights
And left behind a silly song
Instilled into my life.

Ideal Husband

No diamond - no pearl -
No jewel of great value -
Can replace the man that I loved.
No fame - no fortune -
No trip abroad -
Can return his kindness and love.
No satin - no silk -
No fancy lace -
Can restore the tenderness he gave.
No man can ever be -
The ideal husband -
He was to me.

Feeling Blue

I am so tired of feeling blue
All because I yearn for you.
Sometimes I feel a blush of shame
A pride of guilt I cannot explain.
I am not completely clear in mind
As I still carry a burden of pain.
I snugly lay on a sofa of silk
Trying to imagine how you looked.
I hug a pillow - I hug myself -
Then I shrug my shoulders and say,
"I surely will be okay."

Dark Spirits

One foot on the shore -
One foot in the sea -
Simply divides me.
Some days a spray of dew!
Some days a flowering bud!
If only those dark spirits
Would but cease.
I do good deeds - like a cherub -
And I feel like a gallant night
Riding on a huge white dove
With wide wings high above.
One day I hope to be
In a garden of beautiful glory -
Just being me!

Lonesome Here

I am tremendously lonesome here
And my heart is hungry for you.
My home without your love
Is an empty nest of sadness.
I have become a slave to grief.
I gather the fruit of my tears
And smother all my fears.
We loved right into the night.
Only my dream and my belief
Can release me
So I can live in harmony.

Man In The Moon

Ancient as the hills
That man in the moon.
He looks very happy
With all those stars up high.
He is close to heaven.
Do you not agree?
Not far from the Big Dipper
With the Milky Way on his side.
Sometimes he looks gray
With the mist of the day.
The man in the moon
Is for lovers right here -
That is why he shines so bright.
Oh! Man in the moon -
Do not forget
To harvest on me a light.

Many Faces

A clown of many faces
Disguised in numerous attire -
A feathered prince with charm
Yet to be desired -
Big bow tie and tattered hat
With sun glasses to match.
Bow to the prince.
Laugh for the clown.
He is here to last.

Life's Parade

I am on life's parade.
I hear the mighty drum.
The bugles blow -
The cymbals clash.
I show my pride and march.
Each step I pace.
I do not waste -
I learned to enjoy each day.
The bell rings -
The voices sing.
Sacred are the relics of joy
To celebrate life with poise.

Death Comes But Once

Death comes but once!
This I believe.
It is a path of golden tresses
With a vine of breathing roses
That skips a beat.
A shadow of air
With wide wings that fly high.
Bells chime and are heard
In a dusty sky.
A vision presented
With great modesty.
Yes! Death comes but once
And brings to all
A lighted spirit of faith -
To guide us to a field of flowers
And to a joyous angelic heaven.

A Memory Of You

Why do you do this?
You always follow me.
A man wore your clothes today.
Do you remember
That bright red and royal blue?
He carried your sweater
As he walked with discretion -
White sneakers upon his feet.
He walked with no worry -
And paused to look around.
I think he noticed me.
He appeared slightly bewildered.
It was not you -
Only a reminder.
No matter where I am
Or what I do -
There is always
A memory of you.

Key To Your Heart

I strolled in the park to dream
And I looked at the old elm tree so strong
As I whispered your name with love.
Morning glories climbed the hill
While lilies in the garden stood so tall.
The dewdrops I saw melted inside of me
Bringing cloudy tears to my eyes.
I will never forget your smile -
Your wit - the wonder of you -
For I still hold the key to your heart.
It is linked to a chain that I carry with me
Like a mother who cradles her child.

Some Day Together

Intimate is the moment when I miss you.
Unhappy is the day filled with sorrow.
My thoughts of you are strong right now.
I wonder if you know that I still love you.
My heart is crushed and I feel so hollow.
I fantasize you being with me - and I see you smile.
Even though you are so very far away -
How I wish I could touch you and share a few words.
I know I have moved forward.
I tried hard to reach - to feel - to live again.
I finally made it to the top.
Yet sometimes still I live in a world of depression.
I know I must pick myself up and remember
That some day we will be together.

Be There

Be at my side with your spirit.
When all seems to fail, be near.
When my eyes are full of tears
Help make my mind clear.
Just give me a sign
To show me you are here.
Reach out for me -
Somehow - my Dear.

I Write From My Heart

From my head to my heart I do write
And these feelings get way out of sight -
So deep with anxiety -
With memories good and bad.
I pour out my pain
Like a water spout -
To release to you an understanding
Of what I am all about.
My inner agony of suffering
Like a sad and lonely person
Standing in the rain.
No sun - no shadow
A cast of darkened clouds
Deep beneath the words I speak.
A frightening day of misery -
I must - I shall - go on.
No matter what may come my way
I will march - I will strut - I will dance
With no regrets.
I must be strong.
I can - I will - I shall do it today.

I Climbed A Mountain

I climbed a mountain
And I made it to the peak.
My limbs are tired
And my body weak.
Along the way -
No pear trees - no fruit to eat.
It took time, and it was not sweet.
On the way up
There was no one to meet.
I fell down many times -
Heaps of stones dropped on me -
But I always got up on bended knee
And carried on to make that peak.
Now here I am on top of a mountain
And I get a gold medal just for trying.
I always knew I would make it
Because of my love for you
And the strong faith in me.

With Your Eyes

Look at life with your opened eyes -
Be sincere - no unmeaning words to hear.
Be truthful - be strong -
Never gaze at someone too long.
Life's battles must be fought
With gracious thoughts.
Share your spirit - use your wisdom -
Be all that you can be.
Follow the righteous way -
Do not veer or stray -
And give your love away.

Bad Days

It is alright to feel bad some days -
Once in awhile it will hurt.
Just try and say, "Please go away."
Surround yourself with nature's beauty
Or company or tea for two - do not stay blue.
Look at the stars peeping through -
See the beautiful rays from the sun -
New surroundings could be for you.
This will pass and fade
So say hello to a neighbor.
Do not get into a slump
Perhaps a little prayer might do.

Renewed Love

If I should die when I am old,
Will you recognize me?
Will I be older than thee?
Or will I look young?
Into this world above,
Will we renew our love?
Will you be there to greet me?
Should I wear a satin bow?
Or a string of pearls?
Or should I just be me?
When you see me,
Will your arms open?
Or will there be -
A bouquet of scented flowers -
You want to give to me?
Will there be a party?
With family and friends?
I believe our love will be -
A giving grace to each of we.

Faith To Grow

All my thoughts today
Run into a silent tear.
This day so gray
Like a snow-capped hill - far away.
A bitter morning -
Empty - no air with wings.
The winds whirl
Beating on the window sill
Drops of rain.
Seeming lost - even dead -
I am bound still to win.
My love - my hope -
Will not grieve - you are not here.
Yet I do remember holding you, dear.
Keeping the faith to grow
And still clinging to a vine.
No sounds - no sighs -
I will get by.

Two Friends

I have two friends you cannot see -
One stands on the right
The other behind me.
In time of trouble -
In time of fear -
I know they always will be there.
The gift of life I did receive -
To care - to love - to share endlessly.
The sun that shines through deep blue skies
Tells me everything.
The ocean - the shore - the flowers I adore
Give me feelings from deep within.
One friend wears a crown -
The other friend is always around.
When I feel glad or sometimes blue
I know my friends feel this way too.
Each new day - I always say -
Thank you - two - for one more day.

The Only One

You are a sign of strength.
Do you not believe?
A tower to build on -
Sparing your heart of actions -
Giving a glimpse of sunlight
Never darkness.
Am I the only one who can go forward
To cherish the memories
And not to fall or be so alone?
Is this the faith I have
That brings me into a flame
Sparkling into life?
Then I must distance myself
From a journey of pain.
No one can I help -
But make life a precious gift
To shine upon my emptiness.

It Is Gone

My heart has been heavy for so long.
The words you once said forgotten.
I was faithful in our love but it is gone.
I am slipping. Can it be into another's arms?
I dearly cherish the memories -
But I will not be haunted
By the phantom of the years.
I leave you now - do not be weary - be kind.
Watch me carefully - I have no fear.
My hands are warm again.
The field of the beautiful flowers is gone.
Daybreak now brings me happiness
As I walk into the valley of no more tears.

Fence Of Trust

The sun is low - the air is cool.
As I sit beneath a veiling tree,
I wonder if you are sometimes with me.
Blossoms all around -
I gaze into the sky -
Starving for your love - but you are gone.
Knotted branches in the tree -
A reminder of you and me.
We had a fence of trust -
A bond - a wonderful love.
Thankfulness to God - we had it all -
But now you are free.

Be Helpful

Life must count
Each and every day.
Stand for truth -
Be helpful in every way.
Care - share - the needs of others -
Link not to the unbrave.
Do not stress and do not strain -
Aim to rise above the plain.
No choice words -
Just kind smiles -
And laughter will follow you
All of the way.
Walk with delighted joy
With a loving God on your side -
Remembering that you can always
Give your heart away.

Carousel

When I am feeling low,
It is like being on a carousel
Going round and round.
The ride will not stop.
I cannot get off - I feel so lost.
I do so well - I wonder why.
But then comes relapse.
Like being in a boxer's ring,
A punch slaps me down again.
I say - get up - walk ahead -
Push yourself hard.
Turn the table - keep it straight.
Get off the carousel
Before it is too late.

Over The Bridge

No more weeping - Time to move forward -
Gaining some cheerful days.
Time to be ready for oneself - A new joyous day!
Go over the bridge - There is another side.
The bridge will lead you to a crystal lane
Into a valley bright.
No fear - Being there.
Go on to touch - To reach -
To seek - To be yourself so deep.
Feel the breeze - See the colors of the sky.
The people around are so alive.
Go - Take the chance.
Do not deprive those feelings or you will never know.
The other side may be a guiding light.
Stay young - Time marches on.
Look where you are - Look around.
Smell the roses that bloom -
Hear the children sing -
See the mountains so tall - The hills of green -
As sunlight is cast in your eyes.
Do not give in - Strive to be alive.
Do not be alone - Young person of blue.
There are many untried avenues -
Meeting new friends -

Dancing the night away in a stranger's arms -
A little kiss or two - That will do.
Portion out your heart - Do not be afraid.
A tiny hurt - A small teardrop -
Is lighter than your abyss of pain.
Perchance - Some happiness for you!
Would that not be a marvel?
Who might be the one to share?
Cross the bridge and look further ahead.
Could there really be a rainbow?
With a pot of real gold?
Step forward - Go over the bridge -
The other side may be divine.
New beginnings - start today.
This gift of life I then accept
And I shall continue
Living this life gift
From God's abundant love.
It has to be.

Today

So many days have gone away -
What would you say
If you saw me today?
I now have a smile
And I laugh every day.
I feel stronger and happier
Than I did in those gloomier days.
I continued because I cared
And I gave my heart away to share.
This path I walk is no longer narrow
And the light I see is bright.
I learned to give and love again.
You gave me the inspiration to live -
The inspiration I call my gift -
The gift of love that I will keep
And to hold for us while you are asleep.
My turn will come to part
And I know you will be waiting -
For I am not very far from your heart.

Spring

I hear the singing of the birds
The humming of the bees
A pretty song of Spring
My favorite melody.
Poppyseeds - Forget-me-nots
The fragrance of a Lilac -
So green - so clean -
It makes me want to dream.
A honey kiss for lovers to quote -
Babies'-breath rich in my heart -
A long mellow spring day
To complete a wishful thought.

Amazing Perfection

Amazing perfection you find in love.
It can be slow and sly and even shy.
Love is all around the world.
It can even be found in a dolphin of the sea.
It is the cause of quiet restful breathing.
Take a serving of love and you will sleep
Heart to heart with a peaceful keep.
Like perfume from the bud of a rose
Love can be sweet and pleasing.
Love will run smoothly -
As long as the one you love is true.

Satin Night

A midnight walk
On a blue satin night -
Tranquility seems too pure.
Moonbeams shine through the shadows
Of a twilight sleep.
Remembrance of a past love
Fills my heart with joy.
Freshness of the air
Lifts my spirit -
Like days of the love rose.
I do not feel alone - only free -
To wait for the glory
With the glare of the sun -
And for skilled clovers to bloom
With brilliant charm.
Through darkness of midnight -
Through each and every day -
I shall but dwell upon.

Share Your Life

To love again - To make it right.
No wind - No tide - No sea -
Can take away my destiny.
When words are spoken
A banquet song I will hear.
Will you share your life with me, Dear?
To move on - To take a risk.
We will dance and dine -
Sip some wine and feel divine.
To love again - A new romance -
Bells will ring - Lamps will quiver -
My heart will say yes forever.

Love From Above

The night was purple velvet
Upon a harvest moon.
The music we heard
Had the perfect tune.
Our eyes came together
And my heart skipped a beat -
Such a gentleman -
You were discreet.
Your smile was bright
Like a daffodil.
Held close in your arms - I felt no harm -
Only tenderness, contentment
And genuine charm.
This new love sent from up above -
Delicate as a crystal dove.

Hand In Hand

Dance with me till midnight
Kiss me in the rain -
Shower me with love each day
And I will not complain.
Let us walk hand in hand
Along a pretty meadow lane -
For when we are together
I can feel no pain.

A Woman In Love

A woman in love
Can have vanishing beauty.
She will devour you
With her hugs and kisses.
She will make you
Laugh and sing.
She is an angel
With no broken wings.
Her courage and strength
Can be that of a lioness.
But her tenderness can unfold
Both heaven and earth.
She is delicate but knows her own mind.
She is sharp but her moods do swing.
A woman in love
Is like a white dove
In silent flight
Whispering into the night.

Cup Of Life

Renew your faith with a cup of life
Beneath the moonbeams bright.
Your prayers - your kindness - give to thee
Salvation of the dawn with Godspeed.
The flock of stars you wish upon
Can bring you harmony and peace.
Give glory to the heavens above
Singing praise to those we love.

Feelings Of Color

From the yellow light of our lives
For friendship -
To the love of the red rose
For green pastures and hills of hope.
The strength of shining silver
To be forever noble.
Golden rays from sun and moon
To give eternity.
All colors of the rainbow
Soft and full of beauty.
A toast of wine to our time
To give to ourselves.
The azure sky so very high
With snow white clouds of lace -
To be forever lined with love
And so very full of grace.

Look Around

Look around and you will see
The beauty of love surrounding thee.
Like the dawn of the rising sun
The beginning of love is born.
To give - To seek - To be oneself -
Can bring you unity.
To care - To share -
To be always there.
A burning flame deep within your heart -
A small bonus right from the start.
No frowns - No pain -
Just ordinary fame.
Being loved to a day so long -
Must only lead to a simple song.
Look around! Do you not see?
Love is here for you and me.

True Love

True love needs no alterations.
There is no doubt - no darkness -
No cold suspicion.
It is a knot twisted and weaved -
A portrait of man and woman
With a shadow of ferns
And cherry blossoms -
A bonding gift to one another.
Soft air - honey from bees -
Dusk to dawn -
Perpetual love forever.

Is This A Phantasy?

What is love?
Fire with it is cold?
Light when it is dark?
Chilly winds yet the feel of a warm breeze?
A rich colorful rainbow - divinely pale?
Whistling gales at your feet?
A lotus seed in bloom?
A sheer veil of softness -
With a yearning for passion?
Oh Nightingale! Is this a phantasy?
Do I really hear the love notes?
Or a sleeping melody?
Is it a rose in the snow?
Or am I a lost romantic -
In a grave cool with pearls?
Or could I be someone who has loved
And who has truly believed?

Future Time

When I stare into a stream of light
I see your smile and feel you near.
I count the days - then wait -
For your embrace.
Our special time together to love and also share -
Those tender moments of being there.
A secret world we made for us
To grow and learn how far to go -
To bond our friendship beyond
A future time -
Keeping both hearts and heads in mind.
Together with trust and expectations
We gather our wishes in anticipation!
Our hopes and dreams still far away
I know together we will stay.

Magic

Our touch is magic -
Like flowers interlaced with dew
And the touch of soft chiffon.
In a scarlet rose, it is radiance.
In a singing stream, it is music.
It is a sight of loving innocence.
The gentle kiss between our lips -
A perfect vision.
To love - To feel - To want -
To be at your side -
It is magic!

The Candle

The candle's soft glow
And its scent so sweet -
With much love to give
A small fire of peace.
As the slender candle burns
With the mellowness
Of lamps of gold -
Tranquil precious moments
Of beautiful promises
Create love of trust and hope.
Silence the quickening hour -
For the beauty of the night -
Where two hearts beat strongly
Towards a fascinating flight.
Our embracing arms tenderly hold
And give graciously to one another -
A possible bright new future
With love dependent on each other.

Give Love Away

Be not afraid of love in your heart.
It should not be kept a secret.
For love was meant to give away
To someone whose love is present.
Love should not be buried
Nor should it be suppressed.
It is alive and cannot die
For it was intended to be shared.
Through all of life's journeys
It increases and matures -
Like a garden shooting buds
Into the sunshine of each Spring.
Never keep the love that you can give away -
Say the words and then love will begin.
It cannot be purchased for any amount -
There is no special price - only precious worth.
Love is a delicate gift to give -
Not to store away.
To say I love you from your heart -
Will send you on a sweet expedition -
Beyond a past of wishful thinking.

This Little Love

This little love I have inside
Is a rose ready to bloom -
Giving my heart to only you.
Cherished is the special day
My lover says to me -
I am here to stay for you.
Eyes filled with passion
And a laugh that gives me joy -
You speak the words
I have waited so long to hear.
The friendship and adoration we share
Will grow into lasting love -
Because we truly care.

Sweet Flame

We join together our hearts
Hoping never to part -
Sparking like a flash of fire
To bring us a love of total desire.
Each day when you are away -
I dream of the moments
Of your tenderness.
The warmth of your love
I carry with me like a sweet flame.
In the midst of the evening -
However dull or bright -
I always want you here.

Colorful Flowers

A flower is a colorful gift of nature.
Each petal that you touch -
A charming velvety softness -
From the shy purple violet
To the sunshine yellow daffodil -
From the ever-so-loving crimson rose
To the blushing pink carnation.
A bouquet of flowers gathered with pretty ribbon
Can express a love that is to be given
Placed in a vase and sprinkled with time
To grow and to bloom gracefully.
A simple flower alone can give peace
While many flowers can give a celebration of life.
But the Scent of Flowers in a field
Will give solace and comfort
And bring you a beautiful golden light.

Crystal

Silver trees of a cold Winter -
Crystal glass branches
That shine and shimmer
As diamonds scattered in a mine.
To dream and enjoy -
A glorious wonder -
Each tree glittering sterling
Upon a cloudy morn.
As sun rays melt the sparkle
Throughout the day -
Each drop I wish upon.
I take a moment to myself
To eye the frozen trees.
My imagination is just to believe
What nature has given to me.

Blue Butterfly

I walk with peace down a country path
And feel you close to me.
You sent me a sign of a blue butterfly
That flew all about me.
It touched me with mercy
As it fluttered in the sunshine.
You were there with image of power
To give to all a devotion.
The stillness of the quiet breeze -
A cross of faith in the opened meadow -
Bringing us together to love.
Small pretty blue butterfly -
So sweet - so soft in color -
Made me recall
That the splendid Lady in blue
Always inspires our lives
And gives all of us hope too.

Heaven

A veil of blue satin -
Pastel rays with sugar accents -
Mountains of green with herbal scents -
Love with inspiration -
A power of veneration.
Feather-light and delicate to the touch -
A fragrance of dainty flowers always sweet -
A garden of paradise complete -
Never darkness only brightness -
A home of love that is lily-white.

A Short Vision

I went to your grave today.
It was Memorial Day.
I planted pansies, impatiens
And petunias of soft mixed colors -
That added life to your name.
Almost two years have passed -
Yet it seems like yesterday.
I sat on a love bench
Under the tree -
And recalled you to my mind.
I saw you standing in front of me.
You looked happy but it brought me lonely tears.
The vision was brief
Because another man appeared.
He took your place
With just a little space.
He is gentle and has a love for me
In a very special manner.
I looked at your grave
And walked away -
Your face crushed into my heart -
But with thoughts of this new man
And a probable new start.

A Second Time

Love for a second time
Is like a top that spins around.
It makes you feel so very young
Like a newly born shooting star.
To be lucky once more -
Is hard to believe.
He quotes to me: "Do you not know?"
"Do I not show?" "I love you so."
When totally free to love again -
Wait and you will see -
That you can fall in love -
With someone - just like me.

A New Love

Today is the day I put aside
My feelings of passionate love for you.
You cannot caress or embrace me -
Nor kiss or hug me any more.
My heart can now only hold the memories
Of the love that was precious to us.
I am going on - to care and love again -
With the hope that great feelings will come.
I have a need to live fully, to view life anew,
And to love with a freed heart.
So with mild loving thoughts, I now must part.
This new love is so different.
He makes it worthwhile for me to go forward.
He makes me cheerful - always bringing me a smile.
I have a beautiful glow and it shows.
My pain will always be there
And my love for you will never die.
But I am alive here on earth
And I am only human you know.
I want to love and be loved again.
My new beloved is kind and we are good friends.
Because we have a magic love that will grow -
I can now let you go.

A Place For Me

My Dearest Darling! My Sweet Love!
Something is happening to me.
I have to let you go
For I see a future for me.
You have been stolen away
So this has to be.
I am in love with someone new -
But I must admit I still love you too.
I pray for you each and every day
With the hope of seeing you again -
But I need love in my life
And this new beau has love to give.
Though he is always there
I do not know if he will be the one.
What I know is that I feel happy
Because he loves me.
My Dearest Darling! My Sweet Love!
With God's love all around
May you rest in peace -
And please remember -
To keep a place for me.

A Note To God

Oh Lord! My God!
I cannot live without Thee.
I have set forth a journey -
A journey of thanks -
For the light that shines
Upon my life.
I will not question.
Instead, I will praise you
With my thankful words of love.
Heavenly Father! Please lead me
Into a sunny pathway
With a bounty of special grace.
And thank you deeply, Lord,
From the bottom of my heart
For the family and friends
You graciously bestowed upon me.

Index of Poems

To order additional copies of **The Scent of Flowers**, complete the information below.

Ship to: (please print)

Name _____

Address _____

City, State, Zip _____

Day phone _____

_____ copies of *The Scent of Flowers* @ $11.00 each $ _____

Postage and handling @ $2.50 per book $ _____

Rhode Island residents add 7% tax $ _____

Total amount enclosed $ _____

Make checks payable to *Gloria Jean Roy*

Send to: **Gloria Jean Roy**
78 St. Joseph St. #5 • Woonsocket, RI 02895

- -

To order additional copies of **The Scent of Flowers**, complete the information below.

Ship to: (please print)

Name _____

Address _____

City, State, Zip _____

Day phone _____

_____ copies of *The Scent of Flowers* @ $11.00 each $ _____

Postage and handling @ $2.50 per book $ _____

Rhode Island residents add 7% tax $ _____

Total amount enclosed $ _____

Make checks payable to *Gloria Jean Roy*

Send to: **Gloria Jean Roy**
78 St. Joseph St. #5 • Woonsocket, RI 02895